To someone special
MERRY CHRISTMAS

Edited by Helen Exley
Illustrations by Juliette Clarke

I wish you letters and cards
tumbling on to the mat, laughter
and kisses tasting of toffee.
I wish you warmth and shelter,
food and water, peace of mind,
freedom, friendship, love.

Happy Christmas!

≣EXLEY
NEW YORK • WATFORD, UK

WHAT DO I WISH YOU?

The family reunited,
All squabbles set aside,
Food in the larder,
Knocks at the door,
Friendly faces,
Parcels piling up,
Cards from everyone you love,
Nothing forgotten,
Nothing singed,
Laughter, a little silliness,
Hugs, kisses,
Happy memories.
I wish with all my heart that
your Christmas will be all that it
was meant to be –
a little warmth in the depth of
winter, a light in the dark.

CHARLOTTE GRAY, b. 1937

. . .

Other mini books in this series:
To a very Special Daughter   To a very Special Friend
To a very Special Grandmother   To my very Special Love
To a very Special Mother   Happy Anniversary
Wishing you Happiness   To my very Special Wife
To a very Special Dad   To my very Special Husband
To a very Special Son   To a very Special Granddaughter
Welcome to the New Baby

Published in the USA in 1992 by Exley Giftbooks
Published in Great Britain in 1992 by Exley Publications Ltd
Reprinted 1993 (twice). 1994

Illustrations copyright © Helen Exley 1992
Selection copyright © Helen Exley 1992

ISBN 1-85015-322-1

A copy of the CIP data is available from the British Library on request.

Illustrations by Juliette Clarke
Edited by Helen Exley.
Text researched by Margaret Montgomery
Typeset by Delta, Watford
Printed and bound in Hungary.

Exley Publications Ltd, 16 Chalk Hill, Watford, Herts WD1 4BN, United Kingdom.
Exley Giftbooks, 232 Madison Avenue, Suite 1206, NY 10016, USA.

The publishers would like to thank the following for permission to reproduce
copyright material: Doubleday, New York for the extracts from At Wit's End by
Erma Bombeck; The Literary Trustees of Walter de la Mare and The Society of
Authors as their representative for "Mistletoe" by Walter de la Mare; The Franklin
Library for "Conspiracy" by Hamilton Wright Mabie from The Christmas Treasury
and Personal Family Record; Weidenfeld & Nicolson for the extract from Christmas
by William Sansom.

If I gave you a Christmas wish,

I wonder what it would be,

A cuddly elephant, a big posh car, a truck

or a chimpanzee,   .

Or would you ask for the atmosphere,

Of Christmas time all around the year.

JILL WARBURTON, Aged 12

. . .

I heard the bells on Christmas day

Their old familiar carols play,

And wild and sweet

The words repeat,

Of "Peace on Earth, Good Will to Men!"

HENRY WADSWORTH LONGFELLOW (1807-1882)

. . .

At Christmas play and make good cheer,

For Christmas comes but once a year.

from *"A Hundred Points of Good Husbandry"*, 1557

. . .

WHAT IS CHRISTMAS?

It's out of the rut, it's midwinter madness,
it's secrets and hugs and unexpected
visitors and letters from long-lost friends.
It's human beings forgetting to be sensible
and restrained and diet conscious.
It's back to the cave. Food and fire,
laughter and the clan.
I'd *love* another slice of pudding.
Cream? Of course. And just a little
more brandy butter.

PAM BROWN, b. 1928

· · ·

Christmas is not Christmas unless we
enjoy it as children - a little gluttony, a
little silliness - and surprises.

PETER GRAY, b. 1928

· · ·

Christmas should be a time of banked-up
fires, the scent of flowers and wine, good
talk, good memories and loyalties renewed.
But if all else is lacking - love will do.

JESSE O'NEILL

· · ·

LOVE AT CHRISTMAS TIME

To receive a gift, molded from love and sacrifice, selected with care and tied up with all the excitement the giver has to offer, is indeed rare. They don't come along often, but when they do, cherish them.

ERMA BOMBECK
from *"At Wit's End"*

. . .

We expect too much at Christmas. It's *got* to be magical. It's *got* to go right. Feasting. Fun. The perfect present. All that anticipation.

Take it easy.

Love's the thing.

The rest is tinsel.

PAM BROWN, b. 1928

. . .

Sitting under the mistletoe
(Pale green, fairy mistletoe),
One last candle burning low,
All the sleepy dancers gone,
Just one candle burning on,
Shadows lurking everywhere:
Some one came, and kissed me there.

Tired I was; my head would go
Nodding under the mistletoe
(Pale green, fairy mistletoe),
No footsteps came, no voice, but only,
Just as I sat there, sleepy, lonely,
Stooped in the still and shadowy air
Lips unseen - and kissed me there.

WALTER DE LA MARE (1873-1956)

. . .

Forget, forgive, for who may say that
Christmas day may ever come to host
or guest again. Touch hands!

WILLIAM H. H. MURRAY

PREPARATIONS

The proof is not in the pudding but in the fervent
anticipation of it, the counting of the crawling days
before. It is just that the best of Christmas Day itself
all merges into a general brightness, like memories
of the earliest sunny summers which you know to
have been marvellous but whose very blaze of glory
defeats memory: here, in fact, is the blaze of
Christmas being summer in winter again.

WILLIAM SANSOM
from *"Christmas"*

Sing a song of mincemeat,
Currants, raisins, spice,
Apples, sugar, nutmeg,
Every thing that's nice,
Stir it with a ladle,
Wish a lovely wish,
Drop it in the middle
Of your well-filled dish,
Stir again for good luck,
Pack it all away,
Tied in little jars and pots,
Until Christmas day.

ELIZABETH GOULD

. . .

Christmas tree baubles only become valuable when they are veterans, fetched down every year from the attic, a little more worse for wear each year, but worth their weight in memories.

PETER GRAY, b. 1928

. . .

Let the children have their night of fun and laughter, let the gifts of Father Christmas delight their play. Let us grown-ups share to the full in their unstinted pleasures. . . .

SIR WINSTON CHURCHILL
(1874-1965)

. . .

CHRISTMAS IS FOR THE CHILDREN

Never deny the babies their Christmas!
It is the shining seal set upon a year of
happiness. Let them believe in Santa Claus,
or St. Nicholas, or Kris Kringle, or whatever
name the jolly Dutch saint bears in
your religion.

MARION HARLAND

. . .

Not believe in Santa Claus! You might as well not believe in fairies! You might get your papa to hire men to watch in all the chimneys on Christmas Eve to catch Santa Claus, but even if they did not see Santa Claus coming down, what would that prove? Nobody sees Santa Claus, but that is no sign that there is no Santa Claus. The most real things in the world are those that neither children nor men can see. Did you ever see fairies dancing on the lawn? Of course not, but that's no proof that they are not there. Nobody can conceive or imagine all the wonders there are unseen and unseeable in the world.

FRANCIS P. CHURCH (1839-1902)
from *"The New York Sun"*, September 21, 1897

. . .

Santa Claus is not scientific. Nor religious. He's the last touch of magic we will ever know.

CLARA ORTEGA, b. 1955

. . .

CONSPIRACY

For weeks we have all been looking forward to this eventful evening, and the still more eventful morrow. There have been hurried and whispered conferences hastily suspended at the sound of a familiar step on the stair; packages of every imaginable size and shape have been surreptitiously introduced into the house, and have immediately disappeared in all manner of out-of-the-way places; and for several weeks past one room has been constantly under lock and key, visited only when certain sharp-sighted eyes were occupied in other directions. Through all this scene of mystery Rosalind has moved sedately and with sealed lips, the common confidant of all the conspirators, and herself the greatest conspirator of all. Blessed is the season which engages the whole world in a conspiracy of love!"

HAMILTON WRIGHT MABIE (1845-1916)
from *"The Christmas Treasury and Personal Family Record"*

. . .

YAHOO!
CHRISTMAS IS HERE!

When I get up, I
deliberately sleep walk.
I feel my stocking.
Yahoo! I cry, it is
Christmas Day!

RICHARD SUTTON
Aged 10

. . .

A family Christmas
begins before dawn. There
is a creaking, a stumbling, a rustling – and then
the muffled sounds of astonishment, mounting to sh
of triumph. Feet pound along the passage. The bed
suddenly full of elbows and knees and wrapping pape
toys with sharp edges. "He's been. He's been."
And Christmas is under way.

MARION GARRETTY, b. 1917

Everywhere, everywhere, Christmas tonight!
Christmas in lands of the fir-tree and pine,
Christmas in lands of the palm-tree and vine,
Christmas where snow peaks stand
solemn and white.
Christmas where cornfields stand sunny and bright.
Christmas where children are hopeful and gay.
Christmas where old men are patient and gray,
Christmas where peace, like a dove in his flight,
Broods o'er brave men in the thick of the fight;
Everywhere, everywhere, Christmas tonight!

PHILLIPS BROOKS (1835-1893)

. . .

When Christmas comes a tingly comes
over all of me.

IAIN WHITAKER, Aged 12

. . .

SPECIAL PRESENTS

You've decided they must have forgotten – and then there's a phone call.

Now, that's a Christmas present.

PETER GRAY, b. 1928

. . .

You can always tell when you've given the right thing. Instead of, "Oh, thank you, dear - just what I wanted" - you get, "Wow. Oh wow. Oh wow, wow, wow!!"

MARION GARRETTY, b. 1917

. . .

My favorite . . . was a small picture framed with construction paper, and reinforced with colored toothpicks. . . . "Do you like it?" asked the small giver excitedly. "I used a hundred gallons of paste on it." . . .

There were other gifts – the year of the bent coat hanger adorned with twisted nose tissues and the year of the matchbox covered with sewing scraps and fake pearls – and then the small home-made gifts were no more.

I still receive gifts at Christmas. They are thoughtful. They are wrapped with care. They are what I need. But oh, how I wish I could bend low and receive a gift of cardboard and library paste. . . .

ERMA BOMBECK
from *"At Wit's End"*

. . .

Grandmas know the value of lumpiness in Christmas packaging.

JUDITH C. GRANT, b. 1960

. . .

REMEMBER THEM

We open our presents, laugh together, sit down
to eat. But beyond the window - out there
in the darkness - are those for whom Christmas
brings no respite. For them it is another day of
loneliness, fear, imprisonment, hunger, sickness,
homelessness, weariness and war.

To many, even a shabby bedsitter would
be a splendid place - dry, warm, safe and large

enough to house a family.

To many our full larders, our clean water, our health, our peace of mind, our united families are things of which they can only dream. Some knew our world once - and have lost it, or been exiled from it, or had it taken from them. Some have never known anything but fear and poverty and loss. It is right to show our love for one another at Christmas - to share a meal, to exchange gifts, to be happy.

But I wish that we privileged few could hear the voices of all those beyond our windows.

If only now, at Christmas, we could bring them in, share our thoughts and hear their individual stories. For they are not statistics, international problems, drains on government resources. They are individuals, each complex and unique.

Valuable. As we are.

PAM BROWN, b. 1928

. . .

Oh, a wonderful pudding! Bob Cratchit said, and
calmly too, that he regarded it as the greatest
success achieved by Mrs. Cratchit since their
marriage. . . . Everybody had something to say about
it, but nobody said or thought it was at all a small
pudding for a large family. It would have been flat

heresy to do so. Any Cratchit would have blushed to hint at such a thing. At last the dinner was all done, the cloth was cleared, the hearth swept, and the fire made up. The compound in the jug being tasted, and considered perfect, apples and oranges were put upon the table, and a shovel-full of chestnuts on the fire. Then all the Cratchit family drew round the hearth, in what Bob Cratchit called a circle, meaning half a one; and at Bob Cratchit's elbow stood the family display of glass. Two tumblers, and a custard-cup without a handle. These held the hot stuff from the jug, however, as well as golden goblets would have done; and Bob served it out with beaming looks, while the chestnuts on the fire sputtered and cracked noisily.

Then Bob proposed: "A Merry Christmas to us all, my dears. God bless us!" Which all the family re-echoed. "God bless us every one!" said Tiny Tim, the last of all.

CHARLES DICKENS (1812-1870)
from *"A Christmas Carol"*

THE SPIRIT OF CHRISTMAS

Christmas is the most human and kindly of
seasons, as fully penetrated and irradiated with
the feeling of human brotherhood, which
is the essential spirit of Christianity, as the
month of June with sunshine and the balmy
breath of roses.

GEORGE WILLIAM CURTIS (1842-1892)

. . .

God taught mankind
on that first
Christmas day
What 'twas to be a
man; to give, not take
To serve, not rule;
to nourish,
not devour. . .

CHARLES KINGSLEY
(1819-1875)

For somehow, not only at Christmas, but all the
long year through,
The joy that you give to others is the joy
that comes back to you.

JOHN GREENLEAF WHITTIER (1807-1892)

. . .

But I am sure I have always thought of Christmas
time, when it has come round - apart from the
veneration due to its sacred name and origin, if
anything belonging to it can be apart from that - as a
good time: a kind, forgiving, charitable, pleasant
time: the only time I know of, in the long calendar
of the year, when men and women seem by one
consent to open their shut-up hearts freely, and to
think of people below them as if they really were
fellow-passengers to the grave, and not another race
of creatures bound on other journeys.

CHARLES DICKENS (1812-1870)
from *"A Christmas Carol"*

. . .

<u>A SALUTE TO MOTHERS . . .</u>

. . . who have scrimped and saved and shopped and
bargain-hunted,

who have baked and boiled and mixed and mashed,

who have climbed round attics looking for
the box of baubles,

who have stood on chairs to pin up paper chains,

who have stayed up half the night preparing Secrets,

who have made the lists and bought the cards and
sent them out in time,

who have made the costume for Joseph,

who have spent Christmas morning in a daze of
Christmas wrappings and roast potatoes,

who get the brandy to ignite,

who disguise the fact the cat explored the trifle,

who go through the rubbish sacks to find the
missing voucher,

who get the children off to bed,

. who make our Christmas.

PAM BROWN, b. 1928